LEADERSHIP TIPS TO ENHANCE STAFF SATISFACTION AND RETENTION

LEADERSHIP TIPS TO ENHANCE STAFF SATISFACTION AND RETENTION

Robert L. Cooper

To order additional copies of this book, contact:
Xlibris Corporation
1-888-795-4274
www.Xlibris.com
Orders@Xlibris.com
38876

CONTENTS

Introduction

For over twenty-five years, I have dedicated my efforts to assisting organizations to create cultures, where employees can thrive. This means that they become passionate about their work, committed to the organization's vision, and supportive of their colleagues. Experience has taught me a valuable lesson: leaders set the tone for positive change and a work environment that inspires staff to new levels of performance. Content and committed employees provide optimum service for customers and positively impact the bottom line.

In my last book, *Huddle Up—Creating and Sustaining a Culture of Service Excellence*, the discussion involved how each member of an organization must serve each other's needs, thus, optimizing internal and external satisfaction. Leadership plays a key role in setting a positive tone for The Organizational Huddle Process and must continue, each and every day, to earn the trust and respect of the organization's most important asset—the employees who work for them.

This book is a compilation of several leadership tips that I have sent over the last few years to clients and other contacts through my monthly e-zine. If you truly embrace these tips and integrate them into your daily work routine, you will enhance staff satisfaction and retention. My rationale for writing this book is consistent with my overall purpose—to create organizations that deliver excellent business results and do it with heart and passion. These are businesses that we can all be proud of, ones that become employers of choice.

Robert L. Cooper

Motivation

Have you ever thought about what motivates you? You will find that challenging work, the ability to make a positive contribution to the organization's success, recognition for a job well done, and being involved in key decisions are but a few items on the list. What about your employees? What motivates them? One very important insight is that what motivates you are many of the same things that motivate your staff.

Effective leaders create the environment for motivation to flourish. They create challenges for staff to learn and grow. Employees are provided with the opportunity to work on projects that excite their passions. You might say, "What does passion have to do with this? I have a business to run." You are in the people-development business. Your job is to listen to employees and discover what excites them and match their interests to the business needs whenever possible. The key point is to show the desire to serve your employees. That's right, your job is to serve them, not the other way around. The fact that you have taken the time to understand your employee's needs and attempt to meet their needs is a critical step in building loyalty. You may discover that they are not a good fit for their position. If they are a good performer, this may be an opportunity to move them into another position.

Do you observe staff doing things well and then praise them? Many managers are good at catching staff doing something wrong and then writing them up. The manager's office should not be a scary place. Have you ever asked an employee to come to your office to offer sincere thanks? What's important is to create an environment of support—where outstanding efforts are recognized, and mistakes are viewed as opportunities for positive growth.

Are your employees involved in decision making? Do you ask for their opinions? Employees that become involved in decision making, especially when they know their opinion is valued, become committed to the team.

Do you care about your staff as individuals? Do you show support for individuals that are going through difficult times? Loyalty and commitment are very much a function of sincerely caring about people. You cannot and must not fake this. Fundamental to leadership is the ability to truly care about the people you lead. Leadership is about capturing both the hearts and minds of those you lead.

Service Excellence

Leaders have the responsibility of creating and sustaining a culture, where employees provide excellent service to all internal and external customers. The following are several steps that you can take to develop an environment of high customer satisfaction:

1. Model Service Behaviors
    Do you show empathy with others, communicate effectively (especially a good listener), respond to customer needs, and always show respect?
2. Do you and your staff know how customers feel about the service your function provides? Do you respond to problems and ensure they are fixed?
3. Do you involve staff in identifying ways to further improve customer satisfaction? Do your employees see other departments as customers?
4. Have you provided employees with the tools and the opportunities to develop their customer service skills?
5. When you hire a new team member, do you ask questions that establish both technical skills and a service approach?
6. Do you make rounds to ask employees for ongoing feedback relative to obstacles they are facing, make suggestions for improvement, and offer praise for a job well done? You should also look to receive direct feedback from customers whenever possible.
    Effective managers help staff to learn not only the skills but also the importance of delivering service excellence. They coach others to learn and grow from on-the-job experiences. They raise the bar and

praise others for reaching even higher levels of performance. They are willing to periodically roll up their sleeves and do whatever it takes to help the team win. They treat everyone with complete respect in every interaction. They don't blame others for something not going well; they seek to collaborate and fix the problem.

Leading Change

Businesses are constantly experiencing change. We see tremendous changes in technology, reorganizations, layoffs, top management changes, new policies, additional responsibilities placed on staff, and new competitors are but a few examples. The challenge for leaders is how to assist staff to effectively adapt to these changes while accomplishing organizational objectives. This involves managing the human factor. Employees go through a psychological process of transition to come to terms with the change that has been imposed. In some instances, the transition is quick; in others, the process is can be long and painful. Each employee adjusts to change differently and needs to be treated differently. For example, an announcement is made that effective September 1, the accounting offices will be consolidated through the Chicago office. The employees in marketing are having a difficult time handling this announcement. The marketing director struggles to understand why this is happening. The issue here is that employees in marketing may be asking, are we next?

The following are a few tips to assist leaders to manage change and transition:

1. Build commitment for the change. Communicate what is going to change and why the change is necessary. You must also communicate to the best of your ability what is not going to change.
2. Allow two-way communication and encourage questions. You need to keep a true open-door policy.

3. Openly express concerns for those impacted by the change.
4. Ask employees for their help in making the change work; encourage suggestions.
5. Allow grieving, anger, and anxiety.
6. Be tolerant of mistakes, especially when someone is learning something new.
7. Coach and mentor to ensure success.

Creating a Climate of
Open Communications

Effective leaders build an environment where direct, open, and honest communication becomes part of the culture. This allows an organization to focus efforts on delivering exceptional customer and staff satisfaction with increased productivity and operational effectiveness. The following are a few tips to create a climate of open communications:

1. Build trust. Leaders must ensure the words spoken are in alignment with actions taken. This is at the heart of integrity and cannot be compromised.
2. Encourage staff to give input and ideas without judgement.
3. Share information and discuss conflicts openly, assisting others to resolve issues and build positive business relationships.
4. Keep employees informed and explain reasons for change. Be direct and honest at all times. If you do not have an answer, make sure to follow up with staff.
5. Create a real open-door policy; this means having an open mind that allows people to bring comments, complaints, and suggestions.
6. Use a variety of ways to disseminate information. Use bulletin boards, newsletters, department meetings, etc.
7. You need to be an excellent listener. Ask open-ended questions that get staff to communicate what is on their mind. For example, "Bill, what is your suggestion on how to introduce this service to XYZ Corporation?"

8. Create opportunities for staff to collaborate with each other on a regular basis and respond to each other's needs. Are operations and finance in sync with each other?
9. Always remember point number 1.

Passion

Are you passionate about your role as a leader? Do you enjoy mentoring others to accomplish key business goals? Do you truly enjoy modeling behaviors that create a climate of high customer satisfaction? Do you care about your employees and have a strong desire to assist them to reach their full potential? Leaders that have passion own a burning desire to make a difference in the lives of their customers, staff, and the community being served.

If you answered no to any of the above questions, will you be able to maximize business results? Passion is not something you can fake. It's recognizing what gets you up in the morning, and this positive energy has a strong impact on others.

The following are a few suggestions to create passion within yourself and those you lead:

1. Write down those things that would make your job even more fulfilling. If you enjoy being involved in strategic initiatives, see if you can become part of this process. Discuss your vision with your boss by outlining how these ideas will deliver excellent results. Maybe you could even lead this new effort.
2. Ask your staff to identify tasks that they enjoy doing the most. If you have an employee that would like to have more direct involvement with customers, perhaps this can be arranged. You may discover that they have strength in an area that can add great value to the organization. Ultimately, this may mean that they transfer to another department. The important point is both the employee and the organization benefit.

When people are passionate about their work, it does not feel like work; it's pure joy. We need to look beyond the job description to find tasks that truly motivate our team members. People perform their best when contributing to something they truly believe in. Effective leaders find ways to connect people to their passions. Passion leads to high-quality work and optimum job satisfaction.

Delegation

Effective delegation is one of the most important skill sets for any leader. It allows you to focus your time and attention on critical objectives with an eye toward the future. You have more time to develop the skills of others, thus, enhancing staff competency and satisfaction.

The following are several reasons why leaders do not delegate:

1. You believe that you can do it better yourself.
2. The leader lacks confidence in staff.
3. You feel that you are paid to have the answers.
4. It is faster to do it than to have to explain it.

The following are recommended delegation strategies:

1. Describe the project or task and the results expected.
2. Agree on expectations and timetables.
3. Determine any assistance the employee will need to be successful.
4. Define parameters, resources, and authority the employee will have to act.
5. State the amount and frequency of feedback that you expect.
6. Whenever possible, delegate tasks that the employee is fully competent in doing and enjoys.

What is most important is to allow for two-way communication that says, "This is a partnership." It's about providing support to ensure success. This means that the task is completed as planned with the employee feeling a sense of accomplishment and job satisfaction. The best coaches know that their job is to develop the talents of others, give support when necessary, and know when to get out of the way.

Effective delegation frees you up to spend more time on strategic issues, adding even greater value to their organization.

Integrity

Leadership with integrity is critical to the long-term success of any organization. What exactly is integrity in a business context? The following points provide a guideline for leaders:

1. Are you being authentic with yourself and others? Your words and actions must be consistent. Do you do what you say you will do? Do you talk straight?
2. Do you blame others or do you accept responsibility and accountability for results? Effective leaders look for solutions and don't cover up situations.
3. When changing an agreement, do you get acknowledgement from your internal or external customers? For example, if you are to have information to a colleague by Wednesday at 2:00 PM, it is unacceptable to give this at 9:00 AM the next morning unless an agreement between both parties has been established.
4. Are you willing to make the difficult phone call? This is a situation where you did not fulfill a commitment and owe someone an apology. Integrity involves looking in the mirror and being willing to admit when you make a mistake. You, then, take prompt action to ensure others know that you are concerned about the issue.
5. Do you ever execute the messenger? Instead, thank the messenger and take action.
6. Effective leaders are comfortable stating, "I made a mistake," or "It looks like I was dead wrong on this issue."

7. Always seek win-win solutions that take into account the needs of all parties.
8. Effective leaders surround themselves with others who operate from a place of integrity and move away from those who do not.
9. As a leader, you are a role model for others. All employees impact the most important aspect of integrity—organizational integrity. This involves living the mission and values every day. This includes all interactions with customers, the community, vendors, and all staff.

Leaders with integrity promote healthy and positive work environments. Employees respect these leaders and want to work for them. They have the insight necessary to build strong interpersonal relationships. They understand that serving others, respecting others, and being consistent are their job.

Influence

During a seminar that I conducted, a participant asked, "What is the most important attribute of leadership?" My response was, "The ability to influence others to achieve positive results." This involves looking at the difference between management and leadership. One key distinction is that leadership involves positive movement, achieving fundamental change. This, generally, is a result of influencing others to buy into a common vision and approach to achieving the best possible result. It also involves focus, helping others to develop the ability to always add value to the business and customers being served. If it's not a value-added task, then why do it? Management is about maintaining; leadership is about growth.

The key question is will others want to follow? I am not referring to following because you are the boss and have the positional power. This reference is to others' desire to follow. Excellent leaders are surrounded by people who want to follow, are motivated to follow, and, perhaps, are passionate about the direction in which they are going. This will only occur if others trust the leader, respect the leader, and know that the leader truly has both their and the organization's best interest at heart.

Leadership is all about influence. Done well, you create an environment of high internal and external customer satisfaction, with positive business results.

Teamwork

Leaders play a key role in promoting a culture of collaboration and support. The following are a few suggestions to enhance teamwork in your department and throughout the organization:

1. Model what it means to be a good team player. Show support and respect for colleagues (even when they make a mistake), follow through on commitments, and use the word "we," not "I."
2. Give members of your team frequent feedback regarding performance and coach for success.
3. Facilitate decisions made through consensus, ensuring everyone's input is heard and respected.
4. Place emphasis on solving problems rather than pointing fingers and blaming others. Always seek win-win solutions.
5. Keep everyone informed of important issues and changes. Encourage the team to share information with each other.
6. Praise accomplishments and encourage team members to offer praise for each other.
7. Have fun—productivity is higher when individuals truly enjoy their work environment.

Confidence

Former General Electric CEO Jack Welch says, "Effective leaders pump self-confidence into their employees." This concept of confidence is quite complex and develops over time, well before an employee enters the workplace. However, leaders can assist staff to develop a strong sense of self-confidence or erode that confidence. The following are a few tips to build and sustain your staff's confidence level, thus, enhancing performance and results:

1. Focus much of your one-on-one discussions on things your direct personnel are doing well. Encourage and involve them in a dialogue on how to further enhance performance levels, allowing them to assume ownership.
2. Offer constructive feedback in private. These discussions need to focus on, specifically, how your staff member is not meeting a standard. This is important to ensure that you are seen as a leader, who is fair and consistent. If you criticize in public, your staff will feel embarrassed and may shut down.
3. Praise in public with reference to specific accomplishments. For example, "Joan, you did an excellent job on that report for ABC Company. They said your recommendations helped them to reduce costs by 25 percent."
4. When setting goals, involve your staff and make sure the goals are attainable. If a staff member is not competent to achieve a specific goal, they will become frustrated. Assist your employees to develop the competency level required to feel a sense of accomplishment or modify the goal if possible.

5. Let your staff know where they stand at all times. Make sure you are not sending mixed messages. If you need to correct one performance factor, but overall performance is good, let the employee know they are valued.
6. The most important point is having your employees know that you care about them as people and want them to reach their full potential. If not, the other points may not matter.

Power

In many of my workshops, I review the acronym for power to explain several attributes of truly powerful leaders. These leaders do not use positional power to control others. They influence followers by modeling superior leadership characteristics.

Peace—These leaders maintain poise under pressure: always thinking clearly, controlling their emotions, and maintaining respect for others. You can feel their sense of calmness and control, thus, creating a good atmosphere for their team.

Observe—They observe situations from a place of detachment. This means that the leader has the capacity to not getting emotionally involved in the situation or outcome. From this perspective, they can see what is needed to attain a positive result.

Without judgment—They do not look to find fault or blame others. They place their energies on developing others and coaching others to be successful.

Empathy—These leaders show empathy for others, especially when a member of their team is experiencing difficult times. This builds respect and loyalty to both the leader and the organization.

Responsibility—They take full responsibility for everything they do or say. When they make a mistake or fail to meet an objective, they are willing to admit this and apologize when necessary.

Powerful leaders inspire trust, respect, and help create a positive work culture. These inspirational leaders model behaviors for others to emulate. The organization and its customers are the benefactors of this style of leadership.

Choice

The world of business is a place of choice. People choose whether or not they want to follow their leaders. The key word is "want." Do people follow you because they want to or because they have to?

The following are a few reflective questions regarding creating the desire for others to want to follow:

1. Integrity/Trust—Do you demonstrate consistency and believability? Can you be counted on to deliver on your commitments?
2. Support—Do you support others to be successful even if they make a mistake? Do you say thank you for a job well done?
3. Respect—Do you show respect for other's viewpoints even if different from your own? Do you look for the good in your staff and colleagues, assuming the best?
4. Value Input—Do you allow others to offer input, allowing them to take action even if the approach differs from your own?
5. Service—Do people feel that you truly want to serve their needs? Great leaders serve others with support, guidance, compassion, and show their desire to assist others to reach the highest possible levels of success.

One can only be considered a true leader if followers choose to follow. If you take the time to reflect on these questions with a commitment to practicing these principles, you will create the want. If not, you might burn out, spending too much time pushing others to accomplish goals. The leader's job is to ignite passion in others and have them want to go the extra mile.

Customer Number 1

I often ask leaders, "Who is your most important customer?" The answer I am looking for is "My staff." The logic is fairly straightforward. If you treat employees well, and they are competent in their job, they will, in turn, provide good service to your customers. Unfortunately, some leaders miss this important point. They don't see the connection between satisfied employees and satisfied external customers.

The following are a few guidelines to show staff they are customer number 1:

1. Praise often—Acknowledge staff with sincere praise and seek opportunities to do this frequently.
2. Show respect—Treat others as colleagues, not subordinates.
3. Develop competency levels—Ensure staff has the knowledge and tools to be successful. Provide opportunities for future growth.
4. Care for them as people—Show support when a staff member is going through a difficult time.
5. Say thank you—Staff want to feel appreciated. We don't hesitate to thank external customers, why should internal customers be different?

Great leaders see their role as serving their employees, not the other way around. It is through this service to your staff that inspires them to work harder to serve you and all customers. Will your team go the extra mile for you? If not, it's probably because they are not treated as customer number 1.

Lessons from Geese

In many of my workshops, I show a powerful two-minute video called Lessons from Geese. Effective leaders can apply these lessons to build highly effective and productive work groups. The following are the lessons followed by tips for leaders:

1. People who share a sense of community can help each other get where they are going more easily, because they are traveling on the trust of one another.
2. If we have as much sense as geese, we stay in formation with those headed where we want to go. We are willing to accept their help and give help to others because they are traveling on the trust of one another.
3. It pays to take turns doing the hard tasks. We should respect and protect each other's unique arrangement of skills, capabilities, talents, and resources.
4. We need to make sure our honking is encouraging. In groups where there is encouragement, production is much greater. Individual empowerment results in quality honking.
5. If we have as much sense as geese, we stand by each other in difficult times as well as when we are strong.

The following are a few strategies for leaders to apply these lessons:

*   Ensure the team understands departmental and organizational goals and how they contribute to overall success.

- Assist staff to understand each other's challenges and how they can effectively support each other.
- If a team member is having difficulty handling a task, encourage others to pitch in and help. It's important that team members assist without criticizing any colleague.
- Model excellent team behaviors. Always support each other during good and bad times.

People First

In the book *Good to Great*, author Jim Collins discusses how his research team found that one of the key elements in the transformation from being a good to great company is to "get the right people on the bus and the wrong people off the bus." This process of having the right people comes before strategy issues, structure, tactics, etc.

In my experience, I have found that leaders often miss the importance of putting people first. This is one of the reasons many redesign efforts often fail. If you have the right people and provide them with the opportunity to bring your organization to the next level, they will deliver. Often, redesign models prescribe standard approaches that will work in all situations. However, they are often not flexible or adaptable to critical variables such as organizational culture or local market conditions. If you have the right people to evaluate any situation, they will deliver. Our job is to provide them with the opportunity to set direction and be part of building the future.

The following are a few tips to enhance the probability of having the right people on your team:

1. Develop behavioral-based interview questions to find out if the candidate shares your organization's values. For example, if your business places great emphasis on teamwork, ask the candidate to describe how they specifically contributed to developing a teamwork environment in the past.
2. Do not hire because you feel desperate to fill the position. If the candidate does not meet your expectations, wait.

3. Remove people from the team that do not meet your organization's standards. This means taking an honest appraisal of two critical dimensions of performance—technical (results) and interpersonal (*live* organizational values).

4. Ask the following reflective question: if I had the choice of hiring this person again, would I? The answer to this question provides insight into your own values of what it means to have the right people. It is very important that the executive team agree on what these values are, hold each other accountable to modeling these values, and do not compromise.

Those leaders that hire, develop, and retain the right people have taken a big step in becoming an employer of choice.

Strategically Aligned Empowerment

In business, the terms "strategy," "alignment," and "empowerment" are often used as stand-alone concepts. If we put these ideas together, we can empower our employees to resolve key strategic issues that align their ideas with middle and senior management. We ensure that strategies such as enhancing customer satisfaction, revenue opportunities, cost containment, etc., are reviewed by frontline staff with support from direct supervision. Feedback is shared with senior management, thus, creating aligned communications and a true partnership from top to bottom.

I teach a workshop, "Transformation of Manager to Facilitator," that is based on this concept. The idea is that the manager acts as a facilitator, allowing the ideas to emerge from their direct personnel. Employees are empowered to develop prioritized action plans that address critical issues. When done effectively, staff feels a sense of ownership because they had input into the strategies being developed. Plans are communicated with senior management with feedback provided back to staff. As issues get resolved, management can celebrate successes, thus, enhancing staff motivation.

One of the key tasks of leadership is engaging staff in planning and decision making. This allows employees to learn and grow. They develop a true sense of professional satisfaction. We need to develop the critical thinking skills of our team members.

One important step in becoming an employer of choice is to ignite the abilities of frontline staff, those closest to the customer.

Coaching

How would you react to the following scenario?

It's Wednesday, November 30, and you have a critical month-end report to give to your boss by 5:00 PM. One of your direct personnel is responsible for completing this document. At 10:00 AM, this employee meets with you to review the report. You realize that key data is missing.

If this has happened to you, how have you reacted? How do you feel? Is your reaction based on the individual involved or the situation?

These situations are moments of truth. They can either be positive opportunities to learn and grow or leave the employee feeling insecure and frustrated. Great coaches assist staff to learn and grow from mistakes. They make employees feel respected and set up for success. This involves assisting staff to recognize the gap between actual and expected performance with specific actions for success.

The opposite of good coaching is the "red pen." Remember back in grade school, whenever you made a mistake the red pen noted the mistake. In business, pointing out deficiencies without supporting people to be successful creates a climate of fear and distrust. Fear-based environments leave people feeling immobilized, angry, and with low motivation. Supportive cultures make individuals feel secure, relaxed, and motivated to try even harder.

I recommend that you look at every gap in performance as an opportunity to coach for success. Treat every member of your team with respect, helping them to learn and grow.

Accountability

During many of my workshops and consultations, leaders will ask the question, "How do I get my staff to be accountable and take ownership of their performance?"

The following are a few suggestions to assist staff to step into accountability:

1. Do they see the problem? Do they see the gap between actual and expected performance? Effective leaders help employees to see what is required to meet standards.
2. Do employees take ownership of the required change? Staff needs to understand that they are responsible for meeting job standards with the support of their supervisor. This support needs to be enough to enable the employee to be successful but not so directive that the employee is unable to take direction independently. The support provided will be dependent on the employees' ability for each given task.
3. Are your employees afraid to step into accountability? If a staff member makes a mistake, how is this handled? If mistakes become positive learning opportunities, and the employee is encouraged to take action, they will learn and grow. If mistakes are handled punitively, employees will not take action to serve others without your direction.
4. What are the consequences? This gets into the topic of performance management. Are employees recognized for stepping into accountability and providing excellent service to customers? Do they receive ongoing feedback and praise?

This can be a thank-you note placed in the employee's file or a visit from your boss thanking them directly. Not meeting job standards or providing less than acceptable service to customers must be addressed as well, focusing on what it will take to be successful in the future.

5. Perhaps the most important thing a leader can do is model accountability. Let your team see what it means to step into accountability.

Upgrading Talent

Great leaders know that long-term organizational success requires the development of a highly talented and cohesive team. Upgrading talent is not always easy and sometimes very painful. The organization's needs may have grown to a point that someone can no longer meet the job demands. You should assist this individual through performance management to develop the competencies for success. Unfortunately, the employee may just not have the ability to meet expectations. If no other position is available, they may need to be removed from the organization. This must be handled with compassion.

The following are a few suggestions for upgrading talent:

1. How well do you know your people and their interests? You might have people in the organization that possess the talent to assume greater responsibility in other parts of the organization. You should make a comprehensive succession-planning strategy part of how you run the business. This would include providing individualized development plans that assist talented individuals to achieve optimum success.

2. What personal characteristics does your organization value? Do you seek individuals that are self-starters? Does your organizational culture support people that respectfully challenge past practices? Do you prefer employees that follow the commands from above with little input? Great talent is often found in environments that promote innovation, entrepreneurial spirit, risk taking, and career growth. You need to be clear on what talent means for your organization.

3. Jack Welch, the former CEO of General Electric, describes characteristics for talented leaders as the four *E*s and a *P*:

Positive energy—thrive on action, relish change
Energize others—get others pumped up
Edge—make the tough decisions
Execute—get the job done
Passion—excited about their work

Who, in your organization, possesses these characteristics? Do you recruit managers that have these characteristics? These individuals are excellent models for others. They will look to develop and hire people that exhibit the same characteristics.

Talented people want to be on a winning team. If you want to attract and retain talent, then you must play to win. If you accept second best, then what message does that send to others? Top talents want to be the best, they expect to win.

Earning Respect

Which is more important to you as a leader—being liked or respected?

I recall about twenty-five years ago, coming back from a business trip with Bill, the vice president of distribution from a manufacturing company where I was the manager of customer service with thirty-five direct personnel. Bill said, "Bob, some people are going to like you, some will not like you, and others will be in the middle. What's important is that they all respect you. If you can only have one of these, it must be respect."

Over the years, I have come to truly understand Bill's lesson. It is very easy to confuse being liked with being respected. Many business professionals think that if they are liked, respect automatically follows. This is not necessarily the case. Respect must be earned all the time.

The following are a few suggestions relative to earning respect:

1. Deliver results—Don't talk about what you do as much as show what you and your team produce. Hard work alone does not earn you respect, adding value does.
2. Integrity—Be straight and honest in all business dealings; be consistent. See things from the other person's perspective. Always deliver on your commitments.
3. Give credit to others—Let other people receive credit for key accomplishments.
4. Give support at key times—This is especially true when someone is going through tough times, either at work or dealing with a difficult personal issue. Even a termination should be handled with compassion.

5. Treat others with respect—Every employee should be treated with complete respect as individuals and for their contributions. An organization's success is the collective efforts of many people. A sincere "Good morning" or "How are you today?" help create a positive work environment.

Leaders that follow these points will earn the respect of others and, in most cases, will also be liked. The best leaders that I have worked with are willing to take an honest review of each of these points, accept feedback from others, and willing to change course when necessary.

True Empowerment

About twenty-five years ago, I was promoted to the position of customer service manager at a large international manufacturing company. It was during this time that I learned the meaning of "empowerment."

This is a story of a woman named Clara. Clara was responsible for government orders. Clara knew government orders better than anyone else in the organization. One day my secretary said, "Bob, you have a meeting on government orders." I went to this meeting with vice presidents and directors wanting to know specifics on government orders. All I could think about is *Why hasn't Clara been part of these meetings?* The answer I discovered was because she isn't a manager. I decided that from now on, Clara was to attend these meetings, not me. She was the CEO of government orders. She was passionate about government orders. I believed in Clara, trusted her, and felt she deserved to be recognized for the great job she was doing with government orders.

Some of you are probably thinking, *Is he crazy? Didn't he just commit political suicide?* The answer is no! Clara did an outstanding job in answering all the questions on government orders. She was never given the opportunity to share her ideas in an open forum. Several vice presidents commented on how impressed they were with Clara. The benefit was not only did Clara feel a greater sense of pride in her work, others in the department were inspired as well.

The lesson I learned is that true empowerment is a belief system held by the manager. This involves believing that your staff can reach their full potential if you give them the opportunity to shine. You need to first assess each member of your team relative to his or her competence in a specific area. Once you are confident that they know this area of responsibility, treat them as if they are in charge of that area.

Many managers make the mistake of thinking that if they give a staff member power, they lose that power. In my experience, I have found the opposite to be true. This allows the manager to spend more time on other issues and at the same time enhance the motivation of the team. As a result of my empowering style, I was fortunate enough to be selected to head up an employee-involvement program. This allowed me to drive the concept of empowerment throughout the organizational culture. This enabled me to find my passion.

Do you have a Clara in your department? Just look outside your door.

Speak Results

Many years ago, while I was working at an international manufacturing company, the vice president of distribution named Bill, selected me to head up an employee engagement process called Quality Circles. This process involved departmental employees in identifying, analyzing, and solving important operational issues.

One day, I learned a very valuable leadership lesson—speak results. The following story highlights this critical point:

Bill: Bob, how is the quality circle in customer service doing?

Me: Great, Bill, they have had six meetings, attendance is good, and staff seems to enjoy the process.

Bill: But how are they doing, Bob?

Me: The team leader is well prepared, the members are participating, and the quality tools are being used properly.

Bill: What will this project do for our business?

Me: I expect a very positive result.

Bill: How much will the new order entry process save us?

Me: I don't know, Bill, it should be a large sum. We'll have those projections in two or three weeks.

Bill: OK, Bob.

Three weeks later, Bill and I went on a business trip to the Chicago warehouse. Bill was a great leader, a terrific mentor. He said, "Bob, I like you, and I like your style in leading people. From now on, when you are asked the status of a project, you need to speak results, not process steps. Bob, leaders focus on results and always keep their eye on value-added changes. If you learn this lesson, you will become a leader. If not, you will always be seen as a follower."

It's been over twenty years since I worked with Bill, but I never forgot his words. Do you speak about results or process steps? Does your team know which tasks bring the greatest value to your business? Do you mentor others to differentiate between tasks and key results?

Every time I coach a leader, I want to know what value they and their team bring to the business. I do this from a place of total compassion. Bill taught me that those people that focus on tasks and not results become expendable. It's not how hard one works that matters; it's what difference do they make.

Sharing Best Practices

I learned a very valuable lesson many years ago from a former colleague named John. John and I were both customer service managers, supporting different regions of a large international manufacturing company. John's office was directly next to mine. John had over twenty-five years of management experience; I was just promoted into management.

John would periodically say, "Bob, let's get a few members of our respective teams together to learn from each other." We would meet and discuss different approaches to enhancing the service provided to our sales force and customers. John was always willing to share information and was open to new ways of doing things. He modeled for others what true collaboration is all about. John wanted to see me and my team be the most successful we can be. He was a great leader who inspired others to share best practices. This became a way of life within the entire customer service division. Employees were encouraged to share ideas and learn from each other. John helped to create a learning organization.

Great leaders create learning organizations. They pull people from different parts of the organization to learn from each other. They create a culture where employees are encouraged to ask questions, share ideas, and make continuous learning a way of life. They make it safe to say, "I don't know, can you help me?" They reward individuals that are willing to share ideas with others, people who model what teamwork is all about.

I suggest that you look for opportunities to bring people from different parts of the organization to share best practices. Let them know that we need to learn from each other. It might involve bringing managers together to share ideas on how they create a motivating environment for their teams. It could involve bringirg administrative assistants together to discuss different approaches relative to supporting their bosses. What's important is that you inspire others to collaborate in an open, honest, and supportive environment.

Sharing best practices assists organizations to enhance productivity, customer satisfaction, staff satisfaction, and overall effectiveness.

I have not seen John in over twenty years. His lesson has had a profound effect on me. I hope his lesson will do the same for you.

Conclusion

Great leaders create environments where people are inspired to learn and grow and reach their full potential. These are supportive and respectful environments. Individuals are recognized for their contributions. Mistakes are seen as learning opportunities. Teamwork is encouraged and appropriately rewarded. Every employee is provided the opportunity to become involved in offering suggestions to improve business operations and service excellence. Integrity is not only a value spoken; it is modeled by all leaders and becomes part of the fabric of the organization.

Enhancing staff satisfaction and retention is a competitive advantage for those organizations that embrace the principles in this book. The starting point on this journey is enlightened leadership. Those leaders that practice these lessons will improve productivity, market share, and become both the organization and employer of choice.

www.ingramcontent.com/pod-product-compliance
Lightning Source LLC
Chambersburg PA
CBHW030011190526
45157CB00015B/2274